S0-CFO-238

UNDERSTANDING THE
BLACK LIVES MATTER MOVEMENT

THE HISTORY OF CIVIL RIGHTS MOVEMENTS IN AMERICA

by Maddie Spalding

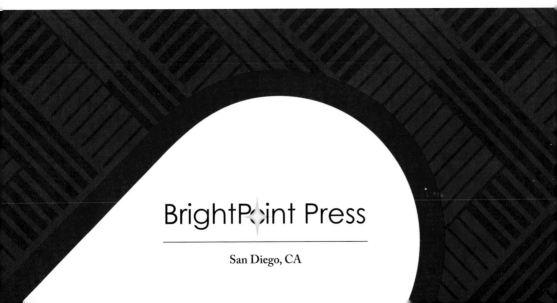

BrightP◆int Press

San Diego, CA

BrightP◊int Press

© 2021 BrightPoint Press
an imprint of ReferencePoint Press, Inc.
Printed in the United States

For more information, contact:
BrightPoint Press
PO Box 27779
San Diego, CA 92198
www.BrightPointPress.com

ALL RIGHTS RESERVED.

No part of this work covered by the copyright hereon may be reproduced or used in any form or by any means—graphic, electronic, or mechanical, including photocopying, recording, taping, web distribution, or information storage retrieval systems—without the written permission of the publisher.

Content Consultant: Derryn E. Moten, Professor and Chair, Department of History and Political Science, Alabama State University

LIBRARY OF CONGRESS CATALOGING-IN-PUBLICATION DATA

Names: Spalding, Maddie, 1990- author.
Title: The history of civil rights movements in America / by Maddie Spalding.
Description: San Diego : BrightPoint Press, 2021. | Series: Understanding the Black Lives Matter movement | Includes bibliographical references and index. | Audience: Grades 7-9 | Summary: "There have been many struggles for civil rights in American history. Black Lives Matter is one of the latest movements, but other groups, including women and Native Americans, have also protested for equality and fair treatment. The History of Civil Rights Movements in America examines earlier movements and looks at how they compare to the Black Lives Matter movement of today"-- Provided by publisher.
Identifiers: LCCN 2020047444 (print) | LCCN 2020047445 (eBook) | ISBN 9781678200749 (hardcover) | ISBN 9781678200756 (eBook)
Subjects: LCSH: Civil rights movements--United States--History--Juvenile literature. | Black Lives Matter movement--United States--Juvenile literature. | African Americans--Civil rights--Juvenile literature. | Indians of North America--Civil rights--United States--History--Juvenile literature. | Women's rights--United States--History--Juvenile literature. | Civil rights--United States--History--Juvenile literature.
Classification: LCC E184.A1 S6956 2021 (print) | LCC E184.A1 (eBook) | DDC 323.1196/073--dc23
LC record available at https://lccn.loc.gov/2020047444
LC eBook record available at https://lccn.loc.gov/2020047445

AT A GLANCE

- Three Black women formed the Black Lives Matter (BLM) movement in 2013. BLM calls attention to racial inequality, including police violence against Black people.

- BLM continues the work of the American civil rights movement. This movement happened in the 1950s and 1960s. Activists protested discrimination against Black Americans.

- BLM activists are inspired by other movements too. The Native rights movement arose in the 1960s. Native Americans asked for equal rights. The US government had taken away many of their rights. This movement remains strong today.

- The women's rights movement also influences BLM. This movement began in the mid-1800s. Women in the United States wanted the right to vote. They gained this right in 1920. Today, activists continue to protest discrimination against women.

- BLM and other movements have used similar tactics. Activists have marched. They have organized sit-ins. They have worked to change laws.

- On May 25, 2020, a Black man died in police custody after a white police officer knelt on the man's neck for several minutes. The man's name was George Floyd. Floyd's death sparked protests. Many people marched in support of BLM.

BLACK LIVES MATTER PLAZA

Congressman John Lewis stood on a rooftop in Washington, DC. He looked down on a street below. Yellow paint spelled out "Black Lives Matter" on the pavement. The letters stretched across two blocks near the White House. The city's mayor had renamed this section of the street Black Lives Matter Plaza.

John Lewis was an activist for civil rights in the 1960s. He later became a congressman for Georgia.

Artists and city workers painted the letters on June 5, 2020. Lewis visited the mural just two days later. The mural had personal importance to him. Lewis was a Black activist. In the 1960s, he had been a leader in the American civil rights movement. This movement's goal was to end racial **discrimination**. Black Lives Matter (BLM) has similar goals.

THE ORIGIN OF BLACK LIVES MATTER

The phrase "black lives matter" first became popular through social media. A Black activist used this phrase in a Facebook post in July 2013. The activist was responding to a court decision. George Zimmerman had been tried in the death of a Black seventeen-year-old named Trayvon Martin. Zimmerman had been

Protesters demanded justice in the death of Trayvon Martin in 2012.

found not guilty. He had killed Trayvon on

February 26, 2012. Zimmerman was a

neighborhood watch volunteer in Sanford,

Florida. Trayvon was walking in the area that

night. Zimmerman thought Trayvon looked

suspicious. Zimmerman later said that they fought. Zimmerman said he shot Trayvon in self-defense. Trayvon was unarmed.

Three Black women started the BLM movement. They did this in response to many incidents of violence against Black people by police and others. Activists used the hashtag #BlackLivesMatter. The movement gained more support after another death. A white police officer named Darren Wilson shot and killed Michael Brown on August 9, 2014. The shooting happened in Ferguson, Missouri. Brown was eighteen years old. He was unarmed.

Alicia Garza, Patrisse Cullors, and Opal Tometi (from left to right) started the BLM movement.

Wilson said that Brown had been reaching for the officer's gun.

GEORGE FLOYD

Violence against people of color remains a widespread issue. Black Lives Matter Plaza got its name after the death of George Floyd. Floyd was a forty-six-year-old

As with protest movements of the past, BLM protesters sometimes confront police officers.

Black man. He lived in Minneapolis, Minnesota. Police arrested him on May 25, 2020. They thought he had used a fake bill at a grocery store. Officers tried to get him into a police car. There was a struggle, and Floyd fell to the ground. Officer Derek Chauvin knelt on his neck for around eight minutes. Floyd repeatedly said, "I can't breathe." He then became unconscious. An ambulance took him to a hospital, where he later died.

Floyd's death caused worldwide outrage. Activists organized BLM protests through social media. They marched in US cities. Protesters honored Floyd and other Black people who had been killed by police.

There is a long history of activism in the United States. Past civil rights movements inspire today's activists. BLM organizers learn from these movements' goals, tactics, and successes.

CHAPTER ONE

WHAT WAS THE AMERICAN CIVIL RIGHTS MOVEMENT?

The American civil rights movement was a protest movement. It gained momentum in the 1950s and 1960s. Activists protested racial discrimination. Black Americans were treated as second-class citizens. Black and white

Before the civil rights movement, it was legal to separate people by race in public spaces. The term colored *was used to refer to some people of color but is now considered offensive.*

people had to use separate facilities. These

facilities included bathrooms and schools.

Black people had to sit at the back of

buses and trains. This type of separation is

called **segregation**.

JIM CROW LAWS

Segregation was more widespread in the South than it was in the North. Still, Black people throughout the country experienced discrimination. Jim Crow laws enforced segregation. Many of these laws emerged after the Civil War (1861–1865). Slavery ended in 1865. Many white Southerners did not want Black people to have equal rights. These rights included education, good jobs, safe housing, and the ability to vote. They feared the idea of Black people having power. For this reason, white officials limited Black people's rights. They created voting

The brutal Civil War, in which many Black soldiers fought, brought slavery to an end.

restrictions such as poll taxes and literacy tests. The literacy tests were designed to make Black people fail. Such restrictions stopped many people from voting.

Black Americans encountered discrimination in other areas too. Many employers refused to hire Black people. Those who did hire Black people often paid them less than white workers. Racial

violence was also widespread. White people

attacked and even killed Black people.

These murders were called lynchings. More

than 3,400 Black people were lynched from

1882 to 1968.

EMMETT TILL

In 1955, Emmett Till was visiting family in Mississippi. Emmett was a fourteen-year-old Black boy. A white woman claimed he whistled inappropriately at her. The woman's husband and her brother-in-law kidnapped Emmett. They murdered him on the morning of August 28. They dumped his body in a river. The two men were tried. They were found not guilty. This injustice angered activists. Like George Floyd's death, Emmett's lynching spurred many people to action.

CIVIL RIGHTS PROTESTS

These injustices continued into the mid-1900s. In 1942, a group of students formed the Congress of Racial Equality (CORE). CORE was based in Chicago, Illinois. Its members organized nonviolent protests. Their strategies included sit-ins. Sit-ins are a type of protest. Many restaurants refused to serve Black people. Black activists entered these restaurants. They sat inside and didn't leave.

In 1954, activists achieved a victory. The US Supreme Court made segregation in public schools illegal. Black students began attending previously all-white schools over the next several years. But segregation in other public places was still legal.

In December 1955, a Black woman was riding a bus in Montgomery, Alabama. The woman's name was Rosa Parks. She was sitting on a full bus. The bus driver told Parks to move to the back so a white passenger could take her seat. She refused to move. She was arrested and jailed. In response, activists formed the Montgomery Improvement Association (MIA). Martin Luther King Jr. led this group. The MIA staged a **boycott**. It urged Black residents in Montgomery to stop riding buses. The

boycott worked. A federal court outlawed

segregation on public buses in June 1956.

But there was still a lot of progress to

be made.

THE FREEDOM RIDERS

The US Supreme Court banned segregation in bus stations in 1960. CORE decided to test the ban. CORE members organized a bus trip. Seven Black people volunteered to go on the trip. John Lewis was among them. Six white people also volunteered. The volunteers called themselves the Freedom Riders. The trip began on May 4, 1961. The activists boarded a bus in Washington, DC. White people attacked them in South Carolina and Alabama. The police did not protect them.

THE MARCH ON WASHINGTON

King and other activists organized a march in 1963. It occurred on August 28. It was called the March on Washington for Jobs and Freedom. Activists A. Philip Randolph and Bayard Rustin organized the march. More than 200,000 people gathered in Washington, DC. They marched in support of equal rights for Black Americans. They asked for an end to segregation.

King delivered a powerful speech. He hoped Black and white people might someday have the same opportunities. King's speech came to be known as the

The March on Washington was one of the biggest protests in history. People fought to end legal discrimination.

"I Have a Dream" speech. John Lewis and other civil rights leaders also gave speeches. Lewis encouraged further action and protests.

CIVIL RIGHTS LAWS

The March on Washington was televised. Millions of people around the world watched the event. Lawmakers noticed. Along with other events, it led to the Civil Rights Act. President Lyndon B. Johnson signed this bill in 1964. It outlawed segregation in public places. It also made employment discrimination illegal.

Activists organized a march in Alabama. They planned to walk from Selma to Montgomery. The purpose of the march was to **advocate** for Black people's voting rights. The activists gathered in Selma on

President Lyndon B. Johnson spoke to the nation on television during the signing ceremony for the Civil Rights Act.

March 7, 1965. Lewis led the march. The activists walked six blocks to the Edmund Pettus Bridge. State troopers were at the bridge. They were armed with clubs and tear gas. They attacked the marchers. News footage of the attack was broadcast around the country. Many viewers were shocked into action. They organized sit-ins

The Edmund Pettus Bridge is still a site of protest today.

and other protests in support of the cause.

Two days after the attack, activists tried

again. State police again stopped them.

A third attempt happened on March 21.

National Guard troops protected the

marchers. The activists were finally able to

reach Montgomery.

President Johnson supported the protesters. He told the American people, "Their cause must be our cause too."[1] On August 6, Johnson signed the Voting Rights Act of 1965. The act banned the use of literacy tests in voter registration.

On April 4, 1968, a white man shot and killed King in Memphis, Tennessee. King's death stunned the nation. Seven days later, Johnson signed the Fair Housing Act into law. This act banned housing discrimination. It said sellers and landlords could not deny housing to buyers or renters because of their race.

INFLUENCE ON BLACK LIVES MATTER

Civil rights activists shaped the nation's laws. Still, racial discrimination remains common today. Police attacked and killed civil rights activists in the 1960s. Police brutality against people of color continues to be an issue today. BLM raises awareness of these injustices. Like past civil rights activists, BLM activists promote nonviolence. They use similar tactics. They have marched and organized sit-ins.

BLM works to advance the causes of the civil rights movement. Sondra Hassan volunteered at the March on Washington.

She reflected on the connection between the civil rights and BLM movements. She said, "It's all been a progression, a movement that just keeps going."[2]

BLM MARCHES AND SIT-INS

On March 18, 2018, two police officers shot Stephon Clark. The police had been called to the scene because someone was breaking car windows in the neighborhood. Clark was a young Black man. He was in the driveway of his grandmother's house in Sacramento, California. Police chased him to the backyard. He had a cell phone in his hand. The police mistook the phone for a gun. Clark died from the shooting. In March 2019, the state attorney general decided not to charge the officers. BLM activists marched in protest of the decision. They also organized sit-ins at the police department.

CHAPTER TWO

WHAT IS THE NATIVE RIGHTS MOVEMENT?

The American civil rights movement inspired another movement in the 1960s. In 1966, Dennis Banks was in a Minnesota prison. Banks was an Ojibwa Native American. Police had arrested him for stealing groceries. Banks had eight children to care for. He stole the food to

Dennis Banks (right) speaks to reporters in 1972.

feed his family. While in prison, he read

about the civil rights movement.

Banks wondered why there was not a

similar movement for Native Americans.

Native Americans also faced discrimination.

They had fewer job opportunities than

white people. Native Americans often could only find low-paying jobs. They also had fewer housing options. Police violence against Native Americans was common. Native Americans were more likely to be arrested than white Americans. Laws tried to erase Native cultures. One law banned Native spiritual ceremonies.

Banks was imprisoned for about two years. He was released in May 1968. Then he approached his friend George Mitchell. Mitchell was also a Native American. Banks asked for Mitchell's help in starting a Native rights organization.

This organization became the American Indian Movement (AIM).

OCCUPATIONS

One tactic Native activists used was occupation. They occupied lands and refused to leave. Occupations were often

THE AIM PATROL

AIM's first action addressed police violence. Activists spoke with the chief of police in Minneapolis, Minnesota. They told him about the police's mistreatment of Native Americans. The police chief did not believe them. In 1968, AIM organized an all-Native patrol. Activists patrolled areas where police targeted Native Americans. They filmed police arresting and beating up Native Americans. They brought this video evidence to the police department.

protests against US government actions.
The government made many agreements
with Native Americans in the 1800s. These
agreements were called treaties. The
government broke many treaties. It also
forced Native Americans to sign unfair
treaties. These treaties pushed them off
their lands. Native Americans had to move
to **reservations**.

Perhaps the most well-known AIM
occupation happened at Wounded Knee.
Wounded Knee is a town on the Pine
Ridge Reservation. This reservation is in
South Dakota. It is home to the Oglala

A memorial marks the site of Wounded Knee in South Dakota.

Lakota tribe. In 1973, some tribal members

wanted new leadership. They felt their

tribal leader was corrupt. Some viewed

him as taking the US government's side

in disputes. But the leader would not step

down. The tribe asked AIM to occupy

Wounded Knee in protest. AIM also went there to protest broken treaties.

Approximately 200 AIM activists went to Wounded Knee. They arrived on February 27. Federal agents surrounded the town. The protest lasted seventy-one days. The agents cut off the electricity and water. There was shooting back and forth. One AIM activist remembered, "They were shooting machine gun fire at us . . . just like a war zone."[3] Agents shot and killed two Native Americans. A federal agent was badly wounded. On May 8, government officials gave in to some of AIM's demands.

They agreed to investigate the broken treaties. AIM activists left. However, the tribal leader remained in power. He was later voted out in 1976.

THE WOUNDED KNEE MASSACRE

In the late 1800s, the US Army attacked and killed many Native Americans. One massacre happened on December 29, 1890. Lakota Native Americans were gathered near Wounded Knee Creek. This creek is in South Dakota. The army surrounded the Lakota people. The troops shot and killed at least 150 Native Americans. Some historians think the death toll was even higher. They estimate that 300 Native Americans were killed. Among them were many women and children. AIM occupied this same historic site in its protest in 1973.

OTHER TACTICS

Native activists protested in other ways too. Banks and fellow AIM leader Russell Means led a protest in 1972. It was called the Trail of Broken Treaties. Activists traveled in cars and buses to Washington, DC. They came from across the country. They reached their destination on November 2. They had many requests for the government. They wanted the government to return some Native lands. They also asked the government to reexamine treaties. Government programs did not provide Native Americans with good health care or

Russell Means was a key leader in Native American activism. He died in 2012.

other opportunities. The activists asked for

better government assistance.

AIM leaders had arranged meetings

with government officials. But the officials

canceled these meetings. Many activists

were upset. They marched to the Bureau of Indian Affairs (BIA) headquarters. They occupied the building. They destroyed some BIA property in frustration. A week later, officials negotiated with AIM. They agreed to consider AIM's requests. They also agreed to review the government's policies.

MARCHES

Like Black civil rights activists, Native activists organized marches. One large-scale march happened in 1978. Activists were protesting eleven proposed bills. The bills would limit Native people's

Marchers on the Longest Walk passed the Pennsylvania state capitol on July 7 on their way to Washington, DC.

rights to hunt, fish, and own land. Activists

also marched for better jobs, housing, and

health care.

The march became known as the

Longest Walk. AIM planned this protest.

The march began on Alcatraz Island

in California. Marchers left this island

in February. Their destination was

Washington, DC. Hundreds of people joined the marchers along the way. They reached Washington, DC, on July 15. Approximately 2,000 marchers entered the capital city. They stayed for a week. They held rallies. Native leaders met with government officials. None of the bills were passed.

THE DAKOTA ACCESS PIPELINE

The Native rights movement continues today. In 2014, a company proposed building an oil pipeline. It was called the Dakota Access Pipeline. It would run from North Dakota to Illinois. Part of the pipeline would travel underneath the Missouri River

Protesters around the country spoke out about the Dakota Access Pipeline.

near the Standing Rock Sioux reservation.

This reservation is in North and South

Dakota. The Standing Rock Sioux rely on

the river for drinking water. They worried the

pipeline would leak or break. Then oil could

spill into the river.

Construction of the pipeline began

in 2016. Activists set up protest camps

near the Missouri River in North Dakota.
Thousands of activists traveled to North
Dakota. Among them were BLM activists.
Black activist Kim Ortiz donated supplies to
a school on the reservation. She explained
why she supported the Native protesters.
She said, "Native Americans have been
through so much. African Americans have
been through so much. . . . We will never
be free until we unite and get free."[4]

The Dakota Access Pipeline protests
received national attention. The pipeline was
completed in June 2017. Activists fought
the oil company in court. In July 2020, a

Activists in Standing Rock lived at protest camps, enduring cold weather.

court ruled in the activists' favor. The court

ordered that a review be done. The review

would look at the pipeline's environmental

impact. The pipeline was shut down and

emptied of oil. Activists hoped their efforts

might shut down the pipeline permanently.

CHAPTER THREE

WHAT IS THE WOMEN'S RIGHTS MOVEMENT?

Many groups of people have faced discrimination throughout history. In the mid-1800s, women could not vote in the United States. At the time, many people thought a woman's place was in the home. They did not think women should

Gaining the right to vote was a key struggle for women in the late 1800s and early 1900s.

be involved in politics. Women organized

and demanded the right to vote. The right

to vote is also called suffrage. Activists

who supported women's suffrage called

themselves suffragists.

THE SENECA FALLS CONVENTION

The first US gathering on women's rights happened in 1848. The gathering was held on July 19 and 20 in Seneca Falls, New York. It was called the Seneca Falls Convention. Approximately one hundred people attended. Most of the attendees were women. Elizabeth Cady Stanton and Lucretia Mott helped organize the gathering. They wrote a document. The document was called the Declaration of Sentiments. It asked for equal rights for women, including suffrage. Stanton and Mott shared the document at the convention. The attendees voted in support of women's suffrage and

other rights.

The convention did not change US laws.

But it drew more people to the cause.

Suffrage was not the only right denied to

SOJOURNER TRUTH

A women's rights convention happened on May 28, 1851. Suffragists gathered in a church in Akron, Ohio. Among them was Sojourner Truth. Truth had escaped slavery. She was an antislavery activist. She also supported women's rights. She spoke about the discrimination she faced as a Black woman. Her speech was published in 1863. Historians do not know if the published version was accurate. Still, it became one of the most famous speeches in US history.

The Women's Rights National Historical Park is in Seneca Falls. Statues there honor the work of women's rights activists.

women. Many US laws treated women as inferior to men. Women had fewer employment opportunities than men. They had less access to education. They could not own property.

THE NINETEENTH AMENDMENT

Suffragists used many tactics to raise awareness of their cause. In January 1917, women began **picketing** outside the White House. They dressed in white clothing and held signs. Police arrested picketers for blocking sidewalks. Some suffragists participated in hunger strikes while in jail. Their jailers force-fed them.

President Woodrow Wilson declared his support for the suffragists in January 1918. He urged the US Congress to pass a women's suffrage amendment to the US Constitution. Some suffragists stopped protesting. The US House of Representatives passed the bill. But the US Senate did not act. The suffragists resumed picketing. Police attacked and

arrested many of them. In September,

suffragists climbed statues in Washington,

DC. They chained themselves to fences.

They set small, controlled fires outside

IDA B. WELLS-BARNETT

Some suffragist groups were segregated. They did not allow Black people to join. Suffragists organized a parade on March 3, 1913. Thousands of women gathered in Washington, DC. They called for a women's suffrage amendment. Ida B. Wells-Barnett participated in the event. She was a Black journalist and activist. The parade's organizers asked Wells-Barnett and other Black women to march at the back. Wells-Barnett refused to do so. She marched among white suffragists.

the White House. Many women went on hunger strikes. Black women were part of the fight for suffrage. But they often faced discrimination within the movement.

The Nineteenth Amendment was adopted in 1920. It gave women the right to vote. Other progress had been made in women's rights too. Women gained property rights. More employers began to hire women. But men were more likely to get higher-paid positions. Gender inequalities still existed. And discrimination continued to prevent women of color from using many of these rights.

Equal pay has long been a key issue in the women's rights movement, both in the United States and abroad.

WOMEN'S RIGHTS IN THE 1960s AND 1970s

A second women's rights movement

started in the 1960s. Women continued to

face discrimination. They were paid less

than men. This difference in pay is called

the gender pay gap. Sexual **harassment**

in the workplace was common. Employers

often fired women who became pregnant. Mothers were expected to stay at home and raise their children.

Women across the country protested for equal rights. They were inspired by the American civil rights movement. They demanded equal pay. They also wanted equal access to jobs and education. They raised awareness of discrimination in the workplace. They asked for an end to harassment and violence against women.

TACTICS AND ACHIEVEMENTS

In 1966, activists formed a women's rights group. It was called the National

Organization for Women (NOW). NOW supported the Equal Rights Amendment (ERA). Activist Alice Paul had written the ERA in 1923. If passed, it would protect women from discrimination.

Women's rights activists organized many types of protests. NOW led a march on August 26, 1970. It became known as the Women's Strike for Equality March. NOW asked women to go on strike for the day. Approximately 50,000 women gathered in New York City. They linked arms. They walked down a busy street. Activists marched in other US cities too. Joyce Antler

NOW continues to play a role in politics and activism today.

participated in the march. She later said,

"The huge number of marchers . . . made a

convincing case that this was a movement

for everyone."[5]

Laws changed as a result of women's

activism. The Equal Pay Act was passed

in 1963. It promised equal pay for women

and minorities. Title VII was passed a year later. It was an addition to the Civil Rights Act. It made gender discrimination in employment illegal. In 1972, Title IX was passed. It prohibited gender discrimination in education.

THE *LADIES' HOME JOURNAL* SIT-IN

On March 18, 1970, activists staged a sit-in. Approximately 100 women entered the office of the *Ladies' Home Journal*. They disliked how the magazine portrayed women. They stayed in the office for eleven hours. They had demands for the editor in chief. They asked him to hire an all-female editorial staff. He did not do this. But he let the activists create part of an issue. A woman was promoted to become the magazine's editor in chief three years later.

Thirty-five states approved the ERA in the 1970s. The approval of thirty-eight states was needed. Then the ERA would become an amendment. The deadline was 1982. But the goal was not met by that year. The ERA did not become law.

THE MODERN WOMEN'S RIGHTS MOVEMENT

Today, activists continue to raise awareness of women's rights issues. They use many tactics to protest. Like BLM activists, they often use social media. Social media can connect activists from around the world.

In 2006, Tarana Burke, a survivor of sexual assault, created a Myspace page to raise awareness. She called her movement "Me Too." #MeToo became a movement on Twitter in 2017. Actresses shared stories of harassment and assault within Hollywood. Other women also shared their stories. Burke urged people to act. She said, "If you're not in the center of change, put yourself there."[6]

On January 21, 2017, the Women's March was held in Washington, DC. Approximately 500,000 people participated. They asked for equal pay

Tarana Burke was the founder of the Me Too movement.

for women. They called attention to gender

discrimination. Donald Trump had recently

been elected as US president. He had

made crude comments about women.

Many women were concerned. They

thought he might work to take away their

rights. Activists around the world organized

similar marches.

CHAPTER FOUR

WHAT IS BLACK LIVES MATTER'S INFLUENCE TODAY?

Past civil rights movements have influenced BLM. John Lewis and other civil rights leaders have lent their support. Lewis's visit to Black Lives Matter Plaza was his last public appearance. He died from cancer on July 17, 2020. He was

After John Lewis's death, his casket crossed the Edmund Pettus Bridge one last time. His legacy continues to shape civil rights activism today.

eighty years old. He encountered racial violence during the American civil rights movement. He saw how this violence persisted. But he still had hope for change. Lewis and other activists continue to inspire today's BLM activists.

MODERN TACTICS AND TOOLS

BLM activists use many tools to spread their message. They apply tactics that were successful in past movements. They also use modern tools such as social media.

Thousands of activists took to the streets after George Floyd's death on May 25, 2020. They organized protests in more than one hundred US cities. They used social media to spread the word. The world was in the midst of a health crisis. A type of virus called a coronavirus had killed hundreds of thousands of people. It caused a dangerous disease called COVID-19. Many marchers

Masks were a common sight at BLM protests in the summer of 2020.

wore masks to prevent the spread of

the virus.

Most of the protests were peaceful.

Protesters called for the arrest of the four

officers involved in Floyd's death. They

also raised awareness of other killings.

On February 23, 2020, two white men had shot and killed a Black man who was jogging. The shooting happened in Brunswick, Georgia. The man's name was Ahmaud Arbery. A few weeks later, a police officer shot and killed a Black woman named Breonna Taylor. The shooting happened in Louisville, Kentucky. Protesters asked for justice. In some cities, artists painted murals on walls and streets. The murals showed support for BLM. Some murals were portraits of Black people such as Floyd. Many included raised fists. This image has become a BLM symbol.

DEFUND THE POLICE

One proposed solution to police violence

is defunding the police. BLM activists have

put forward this idea. Cities set aside funds

for police departments. The funds pay for

THE BLACK LIVES MATTER SYMBOL

A raised fist has become a BLM symbol. BLM activists often raise their fists during marches. They are not the first people to use this gesture. Some Black activists raised their fists in the 1960s. This meant they supported civil rights. In 1968, two Black American runners won medals at the Olympics. They raised their fists during the national anthem. Tommie Smith was one of the runners. He called this gesture a "human rights salute."

Quoted in Margaret Chadbourn, "A Look at the History of the Clenched Fist," ABC News, *May 11, 2016.* *www.abcnews.go.com.*

police activities. Activists think some of these funds could go to social services instead. Social services include counseling and violence-prevention programs. Police officers respond to emergency calls. But many of these calls are for nonviolent emergencies. Officers are trained to use force. They are also trained to respond quickly to perceived threats.

Activists say social services should respond to these calls. These groups are not trained to use violence. They are trained to help with problems such as homelessness. This change could help reduce violence. It could also help people access needed resources and services.

In July 2020, Black activist groups proposed a bill. The bill is called the BREATHE Act. It calls for change in many areas. It would defund the police. The bill

THE "RIGHT TO KNOW" BILL

In 2017, BLM supported a state bill in California. It was called the "Right to Know" Bill. California state senator Nancy Skinner wrote it. The bill was signed into law in 2018. It gave the public access to investigations involving police misconduct. The public could see certain police records. Before the bill was passed, it was difficult to get this information.

would also remove police from schools. It would replace police with counselors. Black activist Patrisse Cullors supports the bill. She is one of the founders of BLM. She said, "We . . . [want] to make sure that the needs of all Black people are met."[7]

THE NEXT GENERATION

Activists of all ages are involved in the BLM movement. Young activists formed the BLM Youth Vanguard in 2015. This group is based in Los Angeles, California. It supports Black children in schools.

Teachers in Seattle, Washington, started the Black Lives Matter in Schools campaign

Many kids have gotten involved in the BLM movement.

in 2016. They wore BLM shirts in their

classrooms on October 19. Families and

students also participated. Many of their

shirts also bore the hashtag #SayHerName.

This hashtag raises awareness of police

violence against Black women.

CONTINUED ACTIVISM

Today, there are more than forty BLM chapters around the world. BLM activists support all equal rights causes. They advocate for women's and immigrants' rights. They speak out against discrimination toward Native Americans. They protest for environmental issues and the rights of **LGBTQ** people. The BLM movement continues to grow. In July 2020, polls showed that about 60 percent of Americans supported BLM. People of all ages and races recognize that change

TIMELINE OF CIVIL RIGHTS EVENTS

July 19–20, 1848
The first US gathering on women's rights happens in Seneca Falls, New York. It is called the Seneca Falls Convention.

August 28, 1963
More than 200,000 people participate in the March on Washington for Jobs and Freedom. This march happens in Washington, DC.

March 21–25, 1965
Martin Luther King Jr. leads activists on a march to advocate for Black people's voting rights. The activists march from Selma to Montgomery, Alabama.

Summer of 1968
Dennis Banks and other Native activists form the American Indian Movement (AIM).

August 26, 1970
Women's rights activists organize the Women's Strike for Equality March.

November 2, 1972
AIM activists march into Washington, DC. They travel from across the country in a protest called the Trail of Broken Treaties. They ask for better treatment from the US government.

April 2016
Native activists set up camp in North Dakota to protest the construction of the Dakota Access Pipeline.

January 21, 2017
Approximately 500,000 people participate in the Women's March.

May 26, 2020
Activists in Minneapolis, Minnesota, begin protesting the police killing of George Floyd.

is needed. They draw strength from the

activists that came before them.

GLOSSARY

advocate

to speak up in support of a cause

boycott

a type of protest that involves refusing to use a service or shop at a business

discrimination

the act of treating people differently based on their race or other characteristics

harassment

an unwelcome and persistent behavior

LGBTQ

a term that refers to lesbian, gay, bisexual, transgender, and queer or questioning people, who are often discriminated against because of their sexuality or gender identity

reservations

plots of land set aside by the US government for Native Americans

segregation

the forced separation of people into groups based on their race or other characteristics

SOURCE NOTES

CHAPTER ONE: WHAT WAS THE AMERICAN CIVIL RIGHTS MOVEMENT?

1. Quoted in Stanford University, "Selma to Montgomery March," *Martin Luther King, Jr. Research and Education Institute*, n.d. http://kinginstitute.stanford.edu.

2. "VIDEO: The Dream, Then and Now: 1963 Marchers Reflect on the 2020 Movement," *National Public Radio*, August 26, 2020. www.npr.org.

CHAPTER TWO: WHAT IS THE NATIVE RIGHTS MOVEMENT?

3. Quoted in Emily Chertoff, "Occupy Wounded Knee," *Atlantic*, October 23, 2012. www.theatlantic.com.

4. Quoted in Ashoka Jegroo, "Why Black Lives Matter Is Fighting Alongside Dakota Access Pipeline Protesters," *Splinter*, September 13, 2016. www.splinternews.com.

CHAPTER THREE: WHAT IS THE WOMEN'S RIGHTS MOVEMENT?

5. Quoted in Sascha Cohen, "The Day Women Went on Strike," *Time*, August 26, 2015. www.time.com.

6. Quoted in Molly Geisinger, "Tarana Burke: Survivor, Not Victim," *Hamilton College*, May 3, 2019. www.hamilton.edu.

CHAPTER FOUR: WHAT IS BLACK LIVES MATTER'S INFLUENCE TODAY?

7. Quoted in Kat Stafford, "Movement for Black Lives Seeks Sweeping Legislative Changes," *Associated Press*, July 7, 2020. www.apnews.com.

FOR FURTHER RESEARCH

BOOKS

Duchess Harris, JD, PhD, *Black Lives Matter*. Minneapolis, MN: Abdo Publishing, 2018.

Duchess Harris, JD, PhD, with A.R. Carser, *Dennis Banks and Russell Means: Native American Activists*. Minneapolis, MN: Abdo Publishing, 2020.

Caitie McAneney, *John Lewis: American Politician and Civil Rights Icon*. New York: Rosen Publishing, 2018.

Siyavush Saidian, *Did the Civil Rights Movement Achieve Civil Rights?* New York: Rosen Publishing, 2019.

INTERNET SOURCES

Kenneth R. Janken, "The Civil Rights Movement: 1919–1960s," National Humanities Center, n.d. https://nationalhumanitiescenter.org.

"John Lewis' Speech: The March," *PBS Learning Media*, n.d. https://tpt.pbslearningmedia.org.

Aleem Maqbool, "Black Lives Matter: From Social Media Post to Global Movement," *BBC News*, July 9, 2020. www.bbc.com.

WEBSITES

Black Lives Matter
www.blacklivesmatter.com

The official Black Lives Matter website gives updates on BLM's actions throughout the country. It also shares the history of BLM.

MNopedia: American Indian Movement (AIM)
www.mnopedia.org/group/american-indian-movement-aim

Learn more about AIM and Native American activists.

PBS: Black Culture Connection
www.pbs.org/black-culture/home

This site shares information on Black American history and important Black figures.

Women's Rights National Historical Park
www.nps.gov/wori/index.htm

The Women's Rights National Historical Park in Seneca Falls, New York, teaches visitors about the history of women's struggle for equal rights.

INDEX

IMAGE CREDITS

Cover: © Harold Valentine/AP Images

5: © a katz/Shutterstock Images

7: © Khalid Naji-Allah/Executive Office of the Mayor/AP Images

9: © Ira Bostic/Shutterstock Images

11: © Jordan Strauss/Invision/AP Images

12: © hkalkan/Shutterstock Images

15: © Everett Collection/Shutterstock Images

17: © Everett Collection/Shutterstock Images

23: © Everett Collection/Shutterstock Images

25: O.J. Rapp/LBJ Library

26: © Michael Scott Milner/Shutterstock Images

31: © Jim Palmer/AP Images

35: © BC Images/Shutterstock Images

39: © s_bukley/Shutterstock Images

41: © Prouser/AP Images

43: © Diego G Diaz/Shutterstock Images

45: © Photo Image/Shutterstock Images

47: © Everett Collection/Shutterstock Images

50: © Zack Frank/Shutterstock Images

54: © Louis.Roth/Shutterstock Images

57: © Benjamin Clapp/Shutterstock Images

61: © lev radin/Shutterstock Images

63: © John Bazemore/AP Images

65: © Michal Urbanek/Shutterstock Images

71: © Justin Katigbak/Sipa USA/AP Images

73: © Red Line Editorial

ABOUT THE AUTHOR

Maddie Spalding is an author and mental health advocate. She has written books on a variety of topics. She lives and works in Minneapolis, Minnesota.